THE STRENGTH IN ME

THE

STRENGTH in ME

OZIOMA JULIET ANAJEKWU

This book was formatted, designed, edited, and published by Heartmenders Magazine Media Inc., New York.

The cover image is a stock image from Pexels.com.
Printed in the United States of America
ISBN 978-1-955915-02-1

For inquiries, contact:
Heartmenders Magazine Media Inc.,
PO Box 312101 Jamaica Avenue,
Jamaica, New York,
NY 11431.
Phone: 1 929-245-7172
Email: heartmendersmagazine@yahoo.com

DEDICATION

This book is dedicated to God Almighty for giving me the enablement and wisdom to write it; without Him there wouldn't be me.

To my parents Late Engr. Jude Ekeocha and Mrs. Angelina Ikolo for bringing me up as the strong woman I am today. To my amiable, ever-supportive, darling husband, Ifeanyi George Anajekwu, for being my rock, counselor, guardian, and adviser, the one I always run to whenever I need comfort or encouragement, and also for being there for me throughout my writing journey.

To my lovely and precious children: Chisom, Ifeanyi Chukwu, Obinna, and Chibuzor Anajekwu, for always being wonderful and supportive.

Finally, to my lovely sisters, families, friends – and everyone who may be experiencing any challenges written in this book.

CONTENTS

ACKNOWLEDGMENT

Many books I have read also influenced the writing of this book alongside my life's experiences. I remain grateful for the knowledge gained reading them and spontaneously used lines and quotes in the pages of this book. At the end of the book is the list of them. I appreciate the encouragement given to me by my family. This book may not have existed without these leaps gotten.

FOREWORD

This is a bare-it-all book; everything is revealed, like peeling a banana to enjoy the meat. Everything! You want money to follow you? But most importantly, do you want to learn to handle what money cannot buy? Things like love and relationships, friendships, etc. Then reading this book is a must. Juliet revealed everything. She gained minds not just from her perspective alone but from realities she quoted from other books or authors. Spirituality is not also cut out from the picture. She showed she was raised with morality and a sense of right and wrong. This author has a strong affinity for the divine. She listens. You can delve into someone's mind by reading them. Juliet is a thinker and a strategist. Multiplying your money like the seeds of a ripened head of sour chop via multiple income streams touched well. And how to be supportive. About mindset, she writes to show that when a car is not running on full power, working on the engine yields the function; when a computer needs debugging, working on the software delivers the result. Therefore, changing someone's mindset yields in how the person behaves. But I have got to warn you. If you feel shy talking about sex, then you may skip Chapter Ten. Juliet talked about it openly as pertaining to marriage and how it can cement the family bond, especially as relating to African women. Everything worth talking about is worth talking about. If I reveal every juice in this book, it may kill your curiosity. Therefore, pick up the book and see your brain reward you by secreting the fantastic four hormones – Serotonin, Endorphins,

Dopamine, and Oxytocin – to make you feel motivated, happy, and sound. This is a feeling you get reading a well-written book like this.

Okechukwu Okugo
Queens, New York
October 2022

PREFACE

This book is a write-up of my experiences and those of my loved ones. This piece is enlightening and touches on various aspects of life.

It is very engrossing yet educative as it guides you through some of life's challenges and how to walk through them.

It will open your eyes to many ways to handle people and situations in life, how to own up to them, and move on.

It will lift your spirit physically and emotionally and help you hold your head high in the middle of challenges in life.

My prayer is for this book to bless and help you in many more ways, so my joy will be complete.

"Our life is a message to the world, let's make it inspiring," Lorrin L. Lee said.

It's always good to face life's challenges and adversities because that is the only push you need to get to your success.

CHAPTER 1

I can do all things through Christ which strengthened me.

CHAPTER ONE

THE STRENGTH IN ME

Strength is defined as one's ability to withstand pressure. This isn't the kind of strength I am talking about but the inner strength that everyone possesses but doesn't realize they have within them. It is a kind of strength that comes to play when life's challenges come knocking at your door. Are you one that has been through tremendous hard times before in life? Are you the one trying to give up or one that has given up on life due to various problems encountered in your lifetime? You need to summon your inner strength and get up because it's not the world's end. You can still get over all your worries, challenges, and sadness, achieve your dreams, and be happy with yourself once again because you have the strength within you.

Life has its definition, but I have my own way of defining it, i.e., facing its challenges as they come and achieving my dreams and goals amidst it all. This mindset has helped me throughout life's struggles, and I am sure if you look at it from this angle, you will embrace her circumstances positively or negatively while moving on.

WHAT IS LIFE?
- Life is a door – Open it.
- Life is a book – Read it.
- Life is a story – Tell it.
- Life is a goal – Achieve it.
- Life is a battle – Confront it.
- Life is a risk – Take it.
- Life is a school – Learn it.
- Life is an opportunity – Grab it.
- Life is a mystery – Unfold it.
- Life is a piece of music – Dance to it!

With the above definitions in mind, you can face any challenge head-on. It is not going to be easy, but you need to work on your mindset to understand that everything lies within you, and you have the enablement to achieve anything you set your mind on, having God by your side too, *"I can do all things through Christ which strengthened* **me." Phil.4:13. KJV.**

Life is not what you plan along the way but what you experience during your journey on this earth. The expectations of everyone around you as you were born, from your parents, siblings, extended families, friends, spouse, etc., vary as one progresses in this journey called life. It starts from your parents hoping and wishing that their children will be the very best, so they can be the envy of all and the pride of the family; they wish you would become that which they have pictured you to evolve so that they can showcase you to the world as a star!

On the other hand, your siblings start a silent competition with you on who impresses the parents more; as such, they try as much as possible to be the best among themselves.

Your extended families are equally looking to know who becomes the star of the family, or the most successful among the siblings, as it is a way of earning respect from everyone in the family or society, and everyone craves that.

On the other hand, there are friends that one has, aiming to be the best and the envy of all in all ramifications, as such they can help either foster a positive competition or harmful one, with no cup or award at the end of the day.

With all these lined up, you will realize that 'LIFE' is a war that you need to fight at every stage; how you fight it now depends on your mindset, either with positive energy to win or with negative energy to lose.

Amidst everything, if you do not set yourself apart and turn away from negative influences, you will start off with an unproductive mindset; this will hinder you from being focused and moving forward in whatever you are doing. A positive mindset and belief in oneself are image boosters and confidence enhancers; you need to have them and let them be a part of you. With it, you can go anywhere in life, meet and dine with the high and mighty and attract positive vibes at all times.

Generally, it is always easy to learn the negatives because that is what is often displayed and played out in our daily lives. Still, when you search within, you will find out that you have more positive attributes. However, the situation in your life, experiences, and challenges have made you push them aside to pick up the negative vibes and attitudes that the world has introduced to you. But never relent in speaking positivity into your life, as that is the only way you can escape your hate and bitterness.

Everyone has different experiences in life due to their upbringing, challenges, traumas, addictions, disappointments, and triumphs.

One cannot judge others based on their beliefs, religion, or way of life because how person A lives and handles their life challenges is quite different from how person B will.

Countries, religions, cultures, and families sometimes influence how one lives their life and, at times, play a positive or negative role in one's way of thinking and treating others as one grows older. Parents need to consider what they say and act in the presence of their kids as they are growing up because, in most cases, how a grown-up turns out is a reflection of what they have been around throughout their growing-up days at their respective homes. As such, one should be weary not to impose their lifestyle on a growing child.

Take a ride with me as we delve into various aspects of one's actualization of their strengths and how they can help you and channel you towards achieving or going for your dreams by working on your mindset to optimize the power in you.

Everyone That Fights Tough In The Ring Must Bear Scars –
Okechukwu Okugo.

CHAPTER 2

Scars That Make You

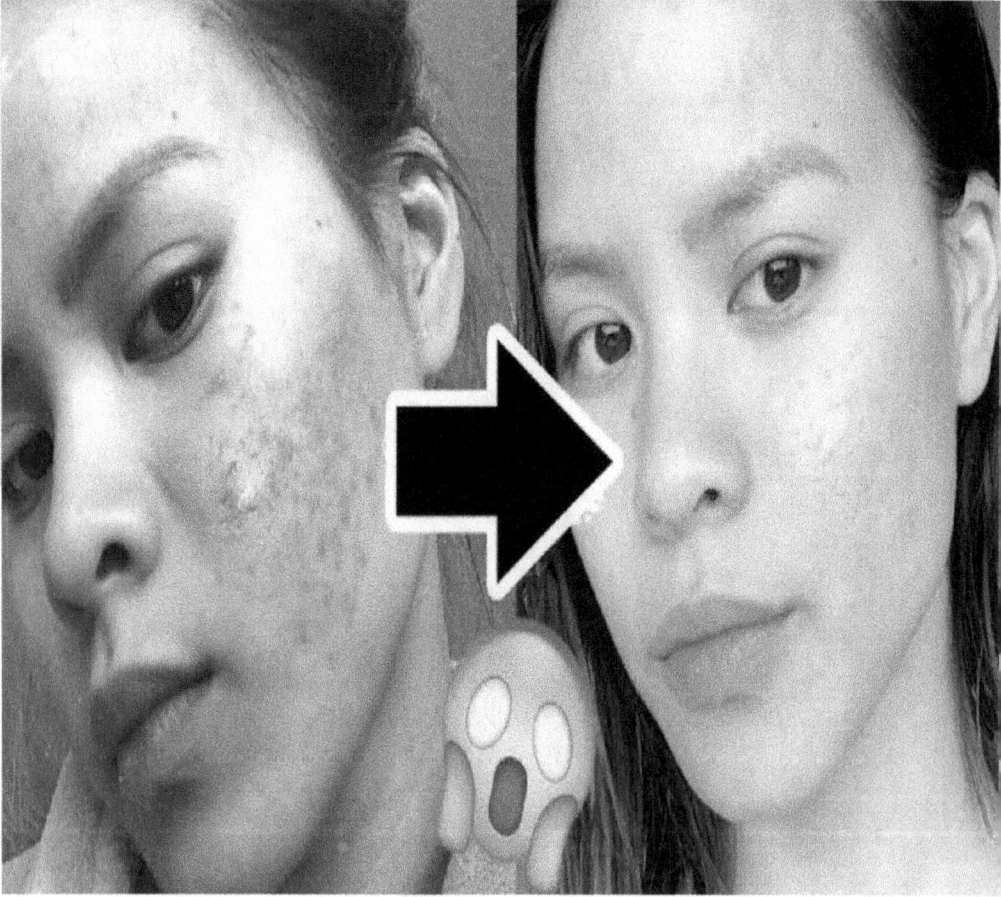

But he was wounded for our transgression and bruised for our iniquities. The chastisement of our peace was upon him and with his stripes, we are healed.

SCARS THAT MAKE YOU

A scar is a mark or a wound on the skin that may make a person feel ugly or imperfect. It can also be the tough road you have been through in life.

Until you begin to see your scar and journey as beautiful, regardless of how you look and whatever you've been through, no one will see it in you. Own up to your scars with pride because that is your story, you are who you are today with those scars, and you have journeyed through life with them, so there will be no you without them, but the scar and imperfections do not make you look less nor uglier but instead, make you unique and beautiful.

The world often judges by one's look or appearance, based on the excellence of some celebrities or people of affluence. But behind fame and fortune sometimes comes emptiness, sadness, and insecurity because even though society sees them as perfect on the outside, there is plenty that makes some of them feel empty on the inside; most regular people think they have it all, but they don't.

Everyone should try as much as possible to be happy with how they look, be it women of color, thick or plump, women with stretch marks, women who have been involved in some accident that left them with some deformity or burns, women with big tummies, etc.

These are some imperfections people tend to work on or try to get rid of. It is good if you can work on some or all of your flaws, but per adventure, you cannot do anything to salvage them, then own up to it with pride because that makes you. Everyone cannot be perfect, but some imperfections make you unique, and only those who look beyond them will see your real beauty.

Many men undergo physical imperfections, such as big tummies and small genitals. But they love themselves with it and still work towards being successful. As they know that when they become successful, women will not be particular about "those things," as they call it. Hence, it's very different for men to manage themselves because they are not interested in physical appearances but in success and wealth.

Most men have a specific focus and hardly care about certain things women do unless someone they love draws their attention to them. Bear in mind that there is always someone out there that will love and accept you just the way you are, so you have to love yourself and know that you are a treasure to someone around you for them to see that, too; self-love is very key.

In this life, no one has it all; amidst all the perfections you see in people, there is also something imperfect about them. That is just how life has made it; they have been strong enough to cover up their imperfections. You also need to own up to your imperfections; you can't deny them, and you can neither run nor forget about them because that makes you who you are.

All relationships go through ups and down, and if one person doesn't want you, another person is out there for you. Don't blame your scars. Anyone can have a failed relationship in the past. Suppose your relationships keep breaking up and dissolving all the time; in that case, there is the possibility that one of you has to work on yourself, as this could signify a projection of past traumas reflecting what is affecting the relationships. Your relationship will not be stable until that trauma is resolved and worked on.

Knowing your worth helps one to move away from unhealthy relationships, and to know your worth, you need to love and respect yourself enough to teach people around you how to appreciate and respect your person.

Not forgetting that it goes both ways; as you love and respect yourself and want people around you to treat you as such, you need to treat people in the same way. If not, then there is a selfish twist to it, and it is not healthy, but you now get the connection. Do to others what you want them to do to you. Respect and treat others well if you want them to show and treat you the same.

CHAPTER 3

Overcoming Heartbreaks

The Lord is near unto them who have a broken heart and saves those of a shattered spirit.

CHAPTER THREE

OVERCOMING HEARTBREAKS

Almost everyone in this life has experienced heartbreak one or more times at a point in life, but how you handle and come out of it strongly depends on the individual. Do you know happiness is the best way to get out of heartbreak? Being happy and doing things that light up your spirit is what helps you come out of a heartbreak fast. When you are heartbroken, don't look for love or companionship in another person immediately. Instead, reflect on all that has happened by listening to cool inspirational music, look back on what happened, and think it through to determine if it was meant to be, or your own mistake, because either way, heartbreak doesn't just happen. Either you are in love with the wrong person and have ignored the early warning signs, or you have done what you aren't supposed to do with the right person. Knowing these things helps determine how to work things out with your future relationship. It enables you to oversee your love life or business, so you don't experience a re-occurrence.

At this point in people's lives, they become vulnerable and would want anything that can ease the pain. Still, the best way to go about it is to do funny or little things, like hanging out with friends, talking to a trusted friend, always smiling, and trying not to be alone for too long, as that may further make you depressed.

You have to understand that not everyone you start a relationship with has the same motives and intentions as you; this should make you guard your heart jealously because when you give it to the wrong person, the pain is devastating. Everyone has their motives/intentions before starting a relationship with you; sometimes, they come to you with the intent to sleep with you and hang out for a while, after which they go for another person. But you, on the other hand, want to build a lasting relationship, thereby putting in your all so that it can work out and maybe, lead to something more serious (business, marriage), not knowing that that is not their intention. You cannot decide how a relationship goes because you are not in control of the other person's feelings or thoughts. Their decision not to be serious with you from the beginning has nothing to do with you, nor does it make the other a bad person; it simply means that you both had different reasons for the same relationship. Sometimes, you talk about what you want in a relationship before being intimate, but as humans, one might not follow the initial arrangement, hurting the other. Sometimes, it's not deliberate because we cannot predict what will happen in the future, as circumstances can make the relationship not work out well. You end up pulling apart, while in some cases, one person may pull out and start another relationship without considering the other person's feelings. This may, in turn, hurt the other person deeply.

Therefore, one should be mindful of who to give your heart to and when you do, make sure it is to someone ready to go the extra mile for you. Peradventure, you give it out to someone who gets your heart broken, don't kill yourself over it, as there is always another person, somewhere, waiting to give you the 100% love you deserve and treat you the way you ought to be treated. So, try to make yourself happy by telling yourself that you deserve better treatment and that if it did not work out well, it simply means it was not meant to be, and the person that lost you has lost a treasure!

It might not be easy, but be firm and love yourself well enough to understand that nobody is worth your tears if they feel you aren't good enough for them. Pick yourself up and move on because it's not the world's end. There are a lot more people out there waiting to love you.

Overcoming Heartbreak: Ways to deal with heartbreak

Accept what has happened, as that is the only way to start healing from the inside.

Do things that will make you happy or things you enjoy doing, such as listening to music, exercising, or meditation.

Evaluate the situation and identify the problems you encountered. Make sure you don't blame yourself for what happened; instead, pick the lessons you have gained from the relationship and work towards it so it doesn't repeat with your next partner.

• Try not to fight the emotions you have for your past partner when they reflect; they will die down gradually as you focus your attention on something else.

• Focus more on growing yourself and attaining greater heights for your highest good.

• Watch as you attract a more loving and respectful partner who knows your worth and treats you right.

CHAPTER 4

Accept your past without regret, handle your present with confidence and face your future without fear.

CHAPTER FOUR

YOUR PAST

Many say that past mistakes sometimes hinder them from focusing well on the future, or negative past experiences deprive them of achieving or pursuing their dreams or goals. Do not let that be your case because you are the architect of your life; you are what you think; you are in charge of what your life ends up with. So, make your life's story more interesting by taking positive control of it.

In the past, most of our parents were not opportune to go to school due to lack of funds or interest, but they were able to train and bring up great minds that, in turn, become great men and women today. Some young men didn't go to school but were determined to be rich and had a lot of educated people working for them because some of them took charge of their lives regardless of the families they came out from or the remotest areas they were born.

So, for everyone that wants to make a difference in their life, you don't have to dwell on the past, but take the bull by the horn and carve a niche for yourself, **"If you can think it, then say you can do it,"** you only have to believe and start something, no matter how small.

A close friend once came to me crying, saying her friends were always laughing at her because she didn't attend university. Whenever her friends talked about their university experiences, and she felt like contributing one way or another, they would hush her up, asking if she had been to the university. This used to hurt her badly, and she decided to come and share her pains with me.

When she told me what was happening, I didn't say anything. I just watched and listened. When she was done, I didn't just go on consoling her, but I made her realize that she could still go back to school to earn her degree and make her friends realize that she could be a graduate. I knew something like that might happen again in the future if not from the same friends, maybe others. So, I told her I was happy they were selling WAEC forms for external students and that we would get her a form because she would return to school. She smiled happily, looking surprised at what I said. The following week, we bought her a form. She took the exams, passed, and got another form for a diploma in UNILAG (University of Lagos). Today, she is a graduate of Business Administration from the same University of Lagos.

So, you see, if you can think about it, with hard work and determination, you can do it, do not let anything hinder you from achieving your dreams. Mind you, the person you share your problems with is very vital as they either give you a lasting solution, leave you or mock you with it; so be wise.

ADVICE: Do not dwell on or blame anyone for your past misfortunes in your life. Instead of moving forward and catching up with new things, acquiring more knowledge or skill to move forward and gather outstanding achievements, you will gradually waste your time dwelling on the past. People say, "Let your shortcomings be a boost for your success in life."
For instance, if your parents are not buoyant enough to send you for higher education, if you have a passion for it, look for a way to help yourself go to school nearby or start a business, build it up and go to part-time school as education has no age limit. You can still go for it at any age if you are determined. By so doing, you would have achieved your dream and made a story to tell your children or the young ones about determination and the will to succeed.

The compounding effects of past trauma:
Trauma is the aftermath of the past. Sadly, we encounter that in our families through what we see, experience, and may be forced to do because of a slight carelessness or neglect by our parents or caregivers.

Some people start experiencing trauma as early as a toddler due to abuse through molestation, which progresses and builds up to more significant and dangerous traumas. Trauma can also occur because of the people around them, what they see and are pushed to do or be part of to act as they belong.

All these build-ups finally affect how some people generally act towards themselves, others, situations, and future endeavors.

So, if you have been faced with many past traumas affecting your way of life now, try to fight it. You can do this by gradually working toward building a better life and future for yourself, so you don't pass that behavior down to your children without knowing it. Certain unwholesome behaviors and generational tendencies arise by not checking or taking care of our traumas and allowing them to rob off on others around us, especially our children.

Your past does not define who you are, as you can mold a better future for yourself regardless of what you have been through. It will be a gradual process, but it is certainly achievable.

CHAPTER 5

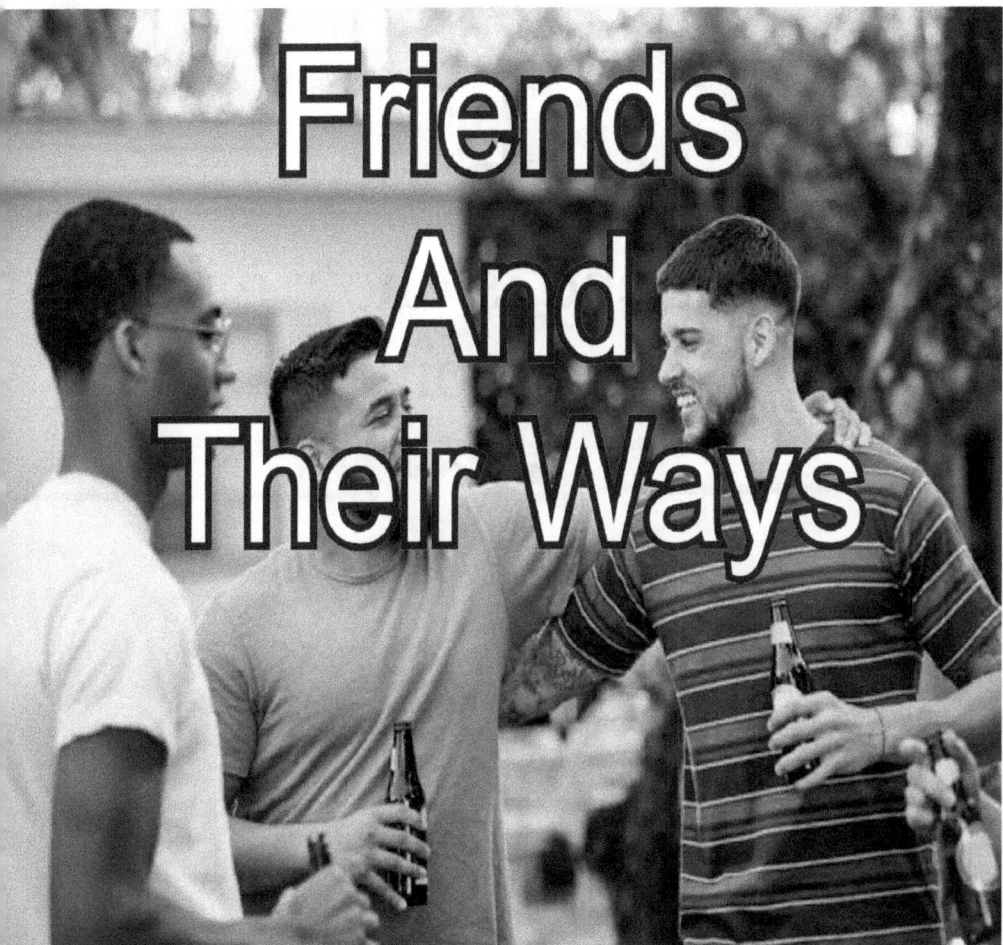

Friends
And
Their Ways

A good friend is one's greatest relation.

CHAPTER FIVE

FRIENDS AND THEIR WAYS

Friends! Friends! Friends!

Having friends is beautiful because you will have some to share your thoughts, problems, and joy with, but if you cannot distinguish between a friend and a foe, you are lost and might end up making the worst choice in life.

We all need to be mindful of the kind of friends we keep, as a lot of them shouldn't even be the kind of people to be with. Most of them are around not because they love you but because of what they can get from you. It can be financial, emotional, or intellectual, i.e., stealing your ideas and discouraging you from a wonderful idea or plan you have. Yes, they can even discourage you from moving on with a beautiful idea you have; in turn, go behind to share the same with someone else, executing it by using another name, and you will never know. So, my advice is to keep your ideas to yourself, execute them till it succeeds and let them hear about your success story later.

Some will want to lure you into doing what you will not normally do, just to know if you have a strong will, but always have them know that you have a mind of your own by saying "No." These things do not go down well with your principle and belief; by so doing, you have shown them that there are boundaries and it's not business as usual when dealing with you.

Be ready to be criticized and pushed aside because you have refused to dance to their tune, but within them, they will know that there is something special about you. They won't admit it nor show you. So always stand your ground and maintain your stand.

39

Before you can be who you are and achieve what you want, you have to be unpredictable, especially regarding friends. You need to tell them what they love to hear, keep the main things to yourself and do things as if you do not have any friends because that is the only way you can save yourself from stress.

Some friends are close to you in some cases just to know what makes you tick and what makes you weak; some use the knowledge or information to better themselves, while others use it to bring you down. The few friends with you genuinely are there so you can grow together financially and in wisdom *"because a good friend is one's greatest relation."*

Bear in mind that in most cases, they don't want drama, and if there is a lot of drama with you or people around you, they tend to leave, not because they don't want to be your friend or love you, but they don't want to be entangled with the drama you have invited into your life. So to avoid such situations, keep very few friends, and avoid crowding yourself with many people. This will help you manage your space and single out those that are just there for the gains but if the good ones still can't see the real you or be with you, let them go so you can make room for those that will understand and love you the way you are when they come.

Be mindful of that friend that always thinks he is better than you. It may be because of their financial stand or material things. Most of them are empty inside and, as such, use those things as a cover-up because they know that you are unique and can achieve anything that you put your heart into. Friendship has got nothing to do with financial strength or material things. No one has it all; as you have some, you may be lacking in other things and may need your friend to help you out with them. Everyone is unique in their own way, and that is how we complement each other, but if they don't understand such a principle, they cannot get the concept of friendship because *"No man is an island."* So, find someone that will love and cherish you the way you love and cherish them for the friendship to work out well.

Do not try to impress your friends by doing what you won't normally do or buying things beyond your means. It is better to make them realize that you operate under the principle of getting your "NEEDS" and not "WANTS." By this, you have them understand that you can't be pressured to spend more than you earn.

Friends should help each other build wealth and gather resources, not encourage you to spend more than you earn unless you have made them believe you earn more than you spend. Then perhaps somebody is deceiving the others.

We should be happy for our friend's successes and achievements, work towards having our own and seek direction or advice from our friend that is doing better in any business or where is necessary so we can achieve the same success. Still, when envy and jealousy come in, it distracts you and makes you lose focus on your own thing. Guard against jealousy.

As much as you want to be far away from "unfriendly" friends, the worst you can do for yourself is to become the person you want to run away from, as this will be a great hindrance, even to you.

Greatness and success are for everyone. The difference is timing. Be focused and consistent in whatever you do, and disregard negative advice. As long as you have a strong conviction in your spirit about what you are doing, it will pay off one day, and those friends that think they are better than you will be seeking your attention. Remember, everyone wants to identify with success.

In friendship, there comes a time when you will need advice or a friend's opinion on an issue or vice versa. It could be for business, marriage, children, etc.

Be mindful because some malicious ones will give you wrong advice, and if you are one that doesn't think over things thoroughly, you may end up making drastic decisions that you will regret later, and when everything turns sour, they will leave you to deal with the problems alone. So, when you know that the friend around you cannot resolve the issue or challenges you are going through, keep it to yourself and pray about it, so you don't add to it by having to deal with people around mocking you after you have shared your problems with someone you thought could be of help.

Remember, *"A burnt child dreads the fire,"* so keep your private thoughts and worries to yourself and take counsel only of your own head. If you are asked now, "What *kind of friend are* YOU?" What will be your answer?

Are you someone who would like to have me as a friend? If you have any hesitation answering this, then you need to re-evaluate yourself to be a better person before being a friend. If I am asked what kind of friend I am now? My answer will simply be: I'm a friend that listens, advises, scolds, intercedes, encourages, pushes, and supports her friends.

I am that friend who will tell you to think about whatever actions you want to take critically so you don t regret them. I am someone that will want you to start a business so you can be independent instead of giving money all the time. I am a friend who will not carry another person's fight on my head just to prove that I am loyal.

I am a friend who will support you to keep pushing even though you are exhausted. I am a friend that will tell you that you are beautiful the way you are and that you have qualities that only you possess though others may not see them. I am a friend that will tell you that you are wrong when you are wrong, regardless of who is involved, so you can work on yourself and be a better person tomorrow. I am a friend that will keep your secret even when we are no more friendly.

Be sensitive and very intuitive with the actions of your friends. Some are close to you just to get the chance to ruin you because they are jealous and wish they could switch opportunities.

There are some good ones out of the bunch. Don't get me wrong, but some friends are foes in disguise, wishing you fail in all endeavors of your life. So be mindful of who you share your inner thoughts with – who you bring to your home and who you allow your children to hang around. The world is so evil these days and age that most people have wicked thoughts toward one another.

CHAPTER 6

And Joseph dreamed a dream
and told it to his brothers: they
hated him more.

CHAPTER SIX

DREAMS

A dream may be a vision, ambition, or storyline one has while sleeping; it may come either as a revelation or warning to the dreamer or, at times, seem irrelevant. On the other hand, a dream is a cherished aspiration, ambition, or idea a person has a burning desire to achieve in their lifetime. Many people have dreams; some they accomplish, while some fade away.

Many people come from humble homes; they work hard at everything and try as much as possible to reach where they hope to be in life, even though the challenges they face along the way tend to make the journey longer and more power-draining time-consuming.

In the world today, most homes are either low or middle-class; parents go to work or their business places to make money that they, in turn, will use to fend for their home (feeding, shelter, school fees, etc.).

As a child growing up, you see the situation your parents are in; you would wish and hope it gets better; as a result, you go to school, study hard, and work hard to make it in life such that your children too won't go through a similar experience. Every child wishes to change the condition of their family by striving to be more successful.

To achieve this, you have to be focused amidst every challenge you find yourself in, knowing that you have to go for what you want regardless. Most successful people in the world today have a long story behind their success. If they weren't persistent in what they were doing, they wouldn't have gotten to the position they are today; this has become a way of life for them since they have built their mindset to do things in a certain way.

For your dreams to come to reality, you need to draw up a scale of preference to know what you need versus what you want. When you can differentiate between the two, you will know what to spend your money on and how to build your resources.

When you are planning to grow in business, you must avoid unnecessary expenses, anything and anyone that can make you spend money you never planned for. If you spend more than you earn, your business can never grow. You also have to look for other income sources to generate a regular cash inflow. Be consistent in what you do; when you do it over time, you will begin to see the result in your finances.

When you encounter challenges while doing whatever you are doing, don't get discouraged; be ready to deal with or handle difficult situations and people you may encounter along the way.

A pastor Sunny Aruwayo, said, *"**Difficult people** are **everywhere, and you meet** them from when you are kids till when you grow up, no matter how good you **think you are to them, they never see anything good about** you."*

He went on to say, *"Most **of them will mock, criticize, discourage, fight, call you names and lie to you because they dislike your guts and don't want you to amount to anything."***

We need to identify them as soon as they start displaying their characters. Some of them were hurt in the past and may now be looking for revenge. Some never want to see others above them, while some are failures looking for people to pull down with them; some are jealous, looking for relevance, while others are immature people needing your help.

Sincerely, you need to identify which category each "difficult person" falls into and, as such, treat them accordingly while moving on with your ambition and dreams.

Being surrounded by different people can only mean that your path crosses theirs because you have leadership potential and a great destiny on the right track. So, it would help if you used all those qualities to advance in life. Everyone has a God-given potential, but each one needs to identify theirs, develop and build it, as this is the only thing you will feel happy and fulfilled doing, even if it pays little or nothing.

Dreams are things you wish to accomplish in your lifetime, but until you work towards achieving them, they start to fade away and die off with time.
Do you have a dream? What are you doing toward actualizing your dreams? Some big dreams require you to take baby steps toward actualizing them. Whatever you want to achieve, you need to start by learning from people that have achieved such. Learn from them and then strategize on how you intend to earn yours.

Be very mindful not to share your ideas or dreams with people or friends around you whom you know have nothing to contribute toward your actualizing the plan, as there is a high tendency that they might steal them without you knowing.

Guard your dreams or ideas in the best way possible because most great and successful people in life become successful that way. They didn't flippantly reveal their best ideas to people before they could actualize them.

CHAPTER 7

"To make money, you need to spend money." Do your research and seek advice from successful people in that line of business to guide you and mentor you.

CHAPTER SEVEN

BUILDING MORE INCOMES

In life, if you want to build wealth, focus on building multiple streams of income. Do a lot of things to generate wealth; this is the only way to stand tall among many people. Remember that you need to work on whatever idea you have and feel strongly about. Avoid talking to everyone about it, as people, most times, are the main reason one doesn't go far because as soon as you share your ideas with them, they will either use it for themselves or discourage you.

They will tell you it won't work and that you are wasting your time. Very few genuine and business-oriented people will advise you to take a shot at it. In reality, before you can succeed in anything, there is a possibility that you will fail a few times.
To build multiple income streams, you need to set money aside to get your new project rolling; remember, "To make money, you need to spend money."

Do your research and seek advice from people who are successful in that line of business to guide and mentor you in your journey; before you know it and with the right people working with you, you will succeed.

If you want to dwell in a particular venture, make sure it is something you are passionate about and not something you want to do just because other people are doing it or you think you can quickly make money from it.

In most cases, the thing that you do passionately is a thing that you will do consistently for a long time, that you probably won't get tired of doing because you enjoy what you are doing; amidst the challenges, you will still continue; because you love what you are doing and in doing such you will end up making money. The thing with life's experiences or building businesses is that if you believe in your craft or dream at the early stage, you are hardly going to see any result, and in most cases, that is when people without passion will drop out.

They get discouraged because they are doing something they neither love nor have passion for. For someone driven, you will see the result in the long run as long as you are consistent at what you are doing, regardless of the discouragement and low or negative feedback along the way. When you end up striving through and making a name for yourself, all the people that thought you were wasting your time or that don't know what you were doing before will come to you for advice.

They will now see you as a success story and want to identify with you. Make a move at doing something you love, take the bold step, and start. It's okay to begin little so you can manage your business well before it grows into a big one. Then, you can start getting professionals to help you manage it.

The main thing is to believe in yourself and that you will succeed in the long run. Building multiple streams of income is something most people will love to have, but it takes a lot of work, focus, and dedication.

I am someone that has gone through a lot to build multiple streams of income; I have done different kinds of businesses, some failed, and some are still functional and doing well. I have also done a series of network marketing; some I didn't go far in, while others took me to different parts of the world. I have learned in my mindset to move ahead in life, to believe I can attain any height I am set to, to be persistent, and to persevere.

Most people, I am sure, can relate to this as they may have experienced such too; it's like a phase in life because as you journey through it, you tend to learn a thing or two that helps you in all you want to do in life.

Robert Collier said, *"Success is the sum of small efforts, repeated day in day* out."

So to be successful in anything you do, you must learn to do it constantly and consistently over time. Have you wondered how some people start a business with very little capital but end up holding up the family and sending their children to choice universities?

It is because they have been consistent in what they were doing and have generated a lot of experience and income. For some, it only has to do with loving what you are doing and doing it well repeatedly, getting better, and being well-known at it.

Thomas Jefferson said, *"Nothing can stop the man with the right mindset from attaining his goal; nothing on earth can help the man with the wrong mindset to attain a goal."*

CHAPTER 8

Being Supportive

"The difference between a successful person and others is not lack   of strength, nor lack of knowledge, but rather lack of will."

CHAPTER EIGHT

BEING SUPPORTIVE

Someone who loves and is always happy to see other people grow or succeed is a builder and supporter. Are you one? If your answer is "yes," then you are a great man/woman. Being a mentor or supporter of growth doesn't diminish your potential; instead, it adds value to your person, and people tend to look up to you because you are building leaders of tomorrow.

Look around; all the people that have gotten to great places in their careers, businesses, or lives generally do not have problems helping or supporting others to grow because that is what made them great. A leader wants to raise or bring up better leaders because they can do great things together. Builders have that in them instinctively because they unknowingly find themselves lifting others and helping them stand on their own in any area they are in.
There is always a sense of fulfillment for someone that supports another and sees them do well in their fields of business or career.

If you often act as if you want to help people, but it isn't your intention, it is better not to give them false hope by acting that way. It is an indirect way of mocking them. It is "very low," so allowing people to find their own way, make their mistakes, and learn from them is better. People that are fond of doing such are usually 'very close;' they know the potential within you yet refuse to acknowledge that there is something good that can come out of it. You often come across these people because they are all around, acting like they are happy to have your back or can take a bullet for you; instead, they are the ones that wish you failure in your quest to succeed in life.

Being a builder/supporter doesn't mean you have to please

everyone; know your capacity and willpower. Inasmuch as you want to carry others along while growing, bear in mind that you don't have to carry nor support all others to the detriment of your finances or business capacity.

Helping others doesn't mean sharing your business ideas with them but allowing them to find their feet in their own business and then showing them what to do and what not to do that got you to your position. Many people are ready to manipulate you into giving them an arm or leg before they can consider you a leader or supporter but try never to be put in a spot where you tend to do the unthinkable to please others and displease yourself. As one that wants to help another, you should be sure the person you are about to help is well-driven in whatsoever he needs you for; otherwise, you will be wasting your time, expertise, and resources grooming such a person.

So, as you identify somebody to help, ensure the person is well-driven in whatsoever they need you for. And they must have some idea of how to execute it. The person must also invest in the business, no matter how little, so that he will commit to it. When you see this as they come to you for support or guidance, you will know where to start and where you want to see them heading after a few years.

"The difference between a successful person and others is not lack of strength, nor lack of knowledge, but rather lack of willpower," Vince Lombardi said.

CHAPTER 9

Love & Marriage

Marriage is honorable in all, and the bed undefiled, but whoremongers and adulterers, God will Judge.

CHAPTER NINE

LOVE AND MARRIAGE

What is love? Love is a romantic feeling you have for another male or female. It is an unexplainable feeling of joy and happiness shared by two people who love one another.

What is marriage? Marriage is a mutual agreement between two individuals to spend their lives together as man and wife. Is there any connection between love in marriage or love and marriage?

Most people marry, hoping their other selves will love and cherish them as they did when they agreed to spend their lives together. Sometimes, it doesn't work out that way, and in some cases, it does. My question now is, why does a marriage break up even before it gets started? This is a question a lot of people find difficult to answer.

In my own opinion, for marriage to stand or fall, it depends on both parties involved. Love is very important in marriage, and there must be understanding, dialogue, and trust to withstand the hurdles therein. It has been the narrative of Africans that women are the ones that can either make or break a marriage.

I don't think it is so, as men can make or break a home. In this journey, it takes two (2) to tangle, and both parties must put in their best because, in marriage, they both should learn to meet each other openly and fully at all times since that is what the union entails.

Whenever there is any misunderstanding, they need to dialogue and iron out the issue, so it doesn't linger for too long. It is also very important for both parties to talk about finances often and ensure that the home is running well; the financial burden shouldn't be on the man alone unless he insists that she should be a "stay-at-home" housewife.

"Men and women in marriage make a vow to love each other affectionately, wouldn't it be better for their happiness if they made a vow to please one another?" Tobias Smollet.
Sex is another part of marriage that is very important; as both parties have their sexual desires, they need to discuss and learn how to satisfy each other's needs often, so they don't end up getting bored of one another.

There should be games and various activities inside and outside the home. They need to play from time to time to spice up their relationship. Find out what tickles your spouse sexually and how to satisfy them, as this is a significant way of stealing their heart. To achieve this kind of satisfaction there has to be an understanding, and the feeling must be mutual, as **"Love is an attempt at penetrating another human being, but it can only succeed if the surrender is mutual."** Octavio Paz said.

In marriage, jealousy is bound to be on both sides, but excessive jealousy destroys. In their quest to be overprotective of the other, most times, either of the two tends to push them farther.

If you observe something peculiar or feel suspicious of anything, it's better to ask your partner about it so they can explain it; that will save you a lot of trouble and stop both of you from doing anything irrational. This is why communication is vital in marriage, as it helps both parties involved to be in control of everything at all times.

On the other hand, some couples have tried these suggestions severally to make happy their partner, but it didn't work, so they decided to go their separate ways since what works for one person may not work for the other. There is always someone out there for everyone; as such, you don't need to kill the other fellow or feel depressed all your life because who you love doesn't love you.

CHAPTER 10

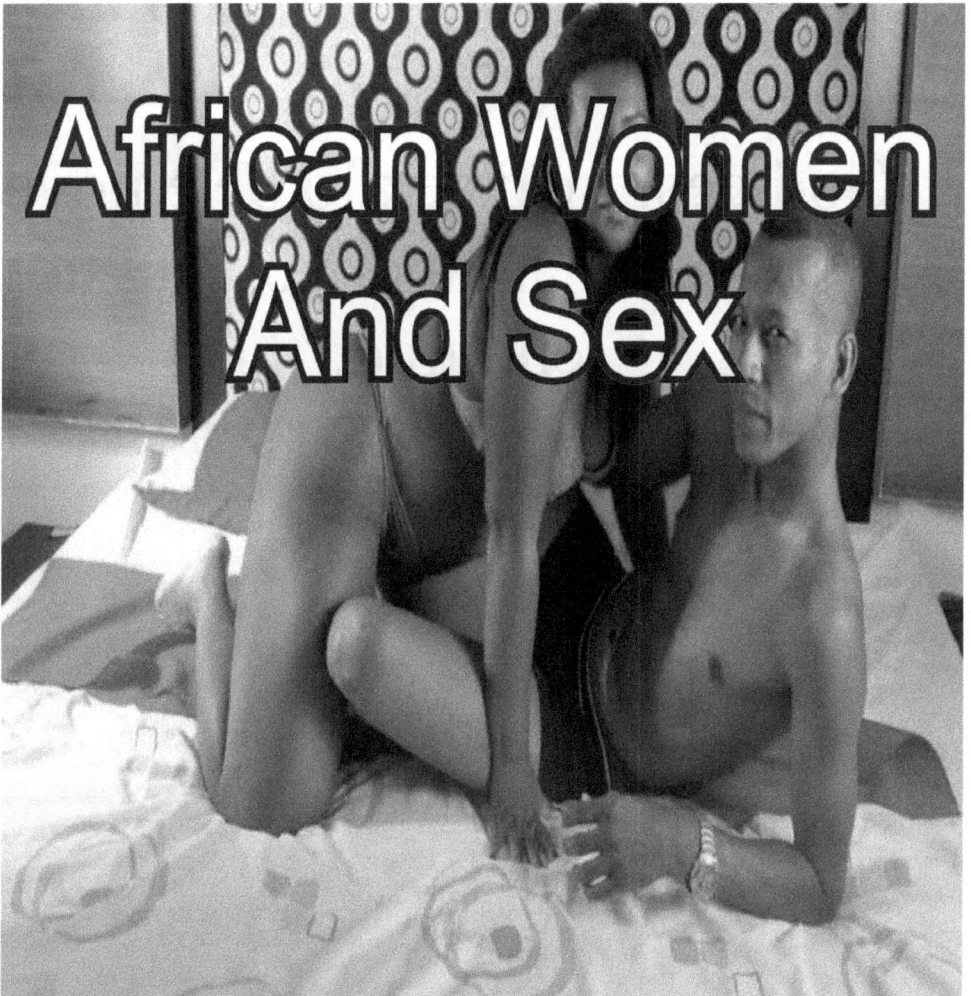

"God designed sex to be enjoyed between man and woman, not endured."

AFRICAN WOMEN AND SEX

I n western countries such as the U.S.A, Europe, Italy, etc., women explore their bodies during sex as they are aware of their sexuality and their men give them maximum foreplay before engaging in it with them. By so doing, both parties enjoy sex. Unfortunately, it's not the same for African women due to culture, tradition, and the general way a woman should portray herself, especially when married.

Sex is the physical mating of man and woman in love and action, which can lead to the reproduction of another human. In most African marriages and relationships, it is always assumed that men enjoy this intercourse more than women. In some cases, women have enjoyed sex, while many have endured it. Satisfaction in sex by a woman depends on her at the time with her partner. A lot of women do not enjoy sex because they do not know how to make their man touch and make them enjoy it. In some cases, the woman who went through genital mutilation has to be handled in a certain way for her to be sexually satisfied.

When a woman is young, sex is very pleasurable and great fun. She tends to make love wildly and carelessly, and she is very adventurous; this makes them enjoy the pleasures of sex better, but they need to understand that as one gets older or married, one might not like those rigorous ways anymore. Some might then prefer it gentle, yet adventurous as the case may be.

Most African women love sex but cannot speak up or communicate effectively to their partners precisely how they want it. If African lady is too wild and adventurous, they tend to be seen as wayward or promiscuous; as such, they suffer an impoverished sex life and sometimes have to use toys to satisfy themselves. This shouldn't be so, as women should be able to enjoy lovemaking and sex just like a man. This is the case of an average African woman, not to talk of one that has her genitals mutilated because of culture and tradition. For such a woman, she may never experience an orgasm in her lifetime because she might not talk about it, lest she would be misunderstood.

Most women derive pleasure only by fondling and touching various sensitive parts or using toys. The size of a man's organ is not a determinant of sexual satisfaction, as satisfying a woman has many other facets.

A male organ has to stand firm with a good erection, with the man knowing how to play well with his woman before entering her, as most women enjoy foreplay. Most men think all women are crazy for big sexual organs, but most times, these men with big organs don't know what to do with them. They display it as if just seeing it is all that makes a woman run wild; if you don't know how to play, massage, and get a woman excited and ready, you have already failed the game before starting, and your big size can't save you. A woman wants to feel needed and be kissed, romanced, touched, softly spoken to, and caressed.

When you do all these, you don't have to do much any longer because you have already gotten her ready, and she is prepared to make love with you.

Most women don't know their G-spot nor reach orgasms during intercourse since they are unaware of their body and sexuality. *What do I mean by G-spot?* The G-Spot is a part of a woman's clitoral network. When stimulating the G-spot, you stimulate the Clitoris, making the woman enjoy sex better. Every woman's G-spot varies; as such, only a woman who is aware of her body can determine where her G-spot is, enabling her to experience maximum orgasm.

A Woman should be free and able to make the man understand precisely how she wants to be touched and made love to, as every woman's body isn't the same. The thing that may turn lady A on may turn lady B off; the same applies to men. As such, there should be sincere discussion in the bedroom. In the business of lovemaking, everyone has the right to be satisfied, and if the man or woman isn't satisfied often, it means they can't be happy with their sexual lives. It means just one party is having total satisfaction while depriving the other of their own. The situation is not as fulfilling as it should be, maybe because they don't communicate well about it, believing both are happy with the outcome.

To enjoy your sex life better, you have to be adventurous and fun-seeking with your partner, as this tends to make the relationship lively and playful, doing things to spice up their lifestyle.

Build a good friend out of your partner because they are the one you spend most of your time with. And in a case where you cannot build a healthy relationship with them, talk about it together and part ways amicably, if necessary, in a way, both of you can still communicate with each other tomorrow.

"Remember everyone that comes in contact with you in your journey through life is there either for you to learn from or to complete your success story."

Sex is magical, and many women enjoy it, especially when bonding with someone who knows their body. Every man needs to get to know his woman and how to satisfy her because if you can meet your woman's sexual needs, you have her to yourself.

Speaking up on what one wants and how one needs to be touched is not something many women are used to doing. They learn to go with the flow and try to adjust to whatever their man tends to do ignorantly to satisfy them. If you don't learn to speak up and direct a man on how to touch you, he will never be able to satisfy you, and that would be something that can potentially affect your relationship.
There should be open dialogue and the ability to try different things to spice up your relationship, as such, doing practical things that tend to enhance the sexual activities in your relationship and marriage.

Some African women don't know how to speak to their partner to satisfy them, which sometimes strains relationships and marriage.

Every man should learn to pleasure their woman before getting down with business, as a lot of women don't even know how it feels to get an orgasm because their man is just out to have sex and sleep off. They won't say anything about it, which would gradually be the beginning and end of their sexual life. There should be no shaming in speaking up in whatever can help spice up your relationship, especially regarding the sexual satisfaction of both partners.

The Reason Why Trees Have Branches Attached To Its Body: To Teach Us The Importance Of Bonding– Okechukwu Okugo.

CHAPTER 11

Bonding

And so, faith, hope, and love abide (faith-conviction and belief respecting man's relation to God and divine things; hope-joyful and confident expectation of eternal salvation; love-true affection for God and man, growing out of God's love for and in us); these three, but the greatest of these is love.

BONDING

Bonding is the allegiance you have with a particular person in a specific way that makes you share anything or something personal, family, or business for a period of time.

It is a special kind of love you cannot have with everyone but that one person your spirit connects with. People are different, and their preferences also differ; as such, one can bond with another with whom you have a sexual relationship, while another person may have a bond leading to marriage. If you have a special connection with a casual friend, for it to last, you have to avoid any sexual relationship, as that may hinder the friendship in the long run. Being in a relationship with someone closer, and they are not comfortable with the bond you have with another friend – you may need to build a stronger bond with your lover to solidify your relationship and remove any form of doubt or suspicion. This makes your love life last longer.

The bond between men is usually more serious than that between women because men always look out for one another except if one is envious of what the other has. On the other hand, the bond between women is mostly hypocritical and unrealistic as most of them, even before getting to know themselves, tend to envy or dislike one another for no justifiable reason – call it "hate at first sight." For women in friendship, when they share a bond, it is often lasting, and you will know because women don't bond quickly as a result of their past experiences in friendship. You will know when you begin to resent your friend or notice any form of withdrawal. Try to work on it, but in a situation whereby the other person involved is not willing to work with you, at that time, you should know that the bond you share may have ended; as such, you need to let it be because to be bonded with someone is a thing of the mind.

If you are connected to any of the few good women out there, you will know that even if you fall out for any reason, you will eventually know. This is because it is a thing of the mind.

Making bonds with one another differ and is based on many things, as some people are more faithful and loyal than others. Some are more serious when it concerns their siblings, spouse, family, friends, parents, or association.

To make a bond in love with another gives you a very good feeling. You will be assured that there's always a person around with whom you can share things, good or bad. For everything you encounter in life, it is very important to have a trusted person nearby that can put you right whenever you are losing it, someone to advise you frankly on how to implement your wonderful ideas without being in any way biased.

There is bonding with business partners, which is a different kind. This is because they share something in common and do things together. This type of bond can exist between a man and a woman and may not be intimate, but because of their closeness, people may misunderstand their kind of friendship, though as time goes on, it can lead to marriage.

"Take All Bonds Seriously, It May Lead To Something Bigger" – Okechukwu Okugo.

CHAPTER 12

People's Space

Have you ever withdrawn for a while from your friends and loved ones genuinely for personal reasons, and they misunderstood you?

CHAPTER TWELVE

PEOPLE'S SPACE

"Space can be defined as an area free and unoccupied. This is a kind of environment someone is looking for to reflect on some needs and to clear their head."

Space in people's lives varies; some people are very particular about their space, while others aren't. This most times has to do with one's upbringing and how they had spent a better part of their lives. People vary in their understanding and ways of life; the reason what you see and how you do the same thing varies one from the other. Sometimes, a person needs space due to stress or personal issues and needs time alone to think and reflect on these issues bottled up in their minds.

A person you love and are close to may decide to stay away for a while; it doesn't mean they don't love or care about you anymore; it simply means they are reflecting on things and finding a way to put their thoughts together. Most people who are not used to this kind of period may not understand it. They may think they are being shut out, even after letting them know why they want to be alone. One needs to grow and understand how their friends or loved ones are and how they act according to the situation they find themselves in, so they won't feel neglected. Also, it helps to build up ways to connect better maturely.

Have you ever withdrawn for a while from your friends and loved ones genuinely for personal reasons, and they misunderstood you? I have had similar experiences in the past. I have had some people who understood while others didn't, even after talking to them about it. Make them understand that you still love them but want to be left alone for that period.

Situations like this arise in marriages and other kinds of relationships, and such requires being left alone; this sometimes helps in relationships where they are always fighting at every slight provocation. Thinking through what is happening and doing your quiet time away from each other helps one decide if the relationship or marriage is worth fighting for or not.

Marriage is an institution you learn from every day, and please remember, for your home to be sweet, learn to love and tolerate each other because love is a flower that turns into sweet fruit in marriage. Often, being repentant, asking for and getting forgiveness makes it sweeter and last forever.

CHAPTER 13

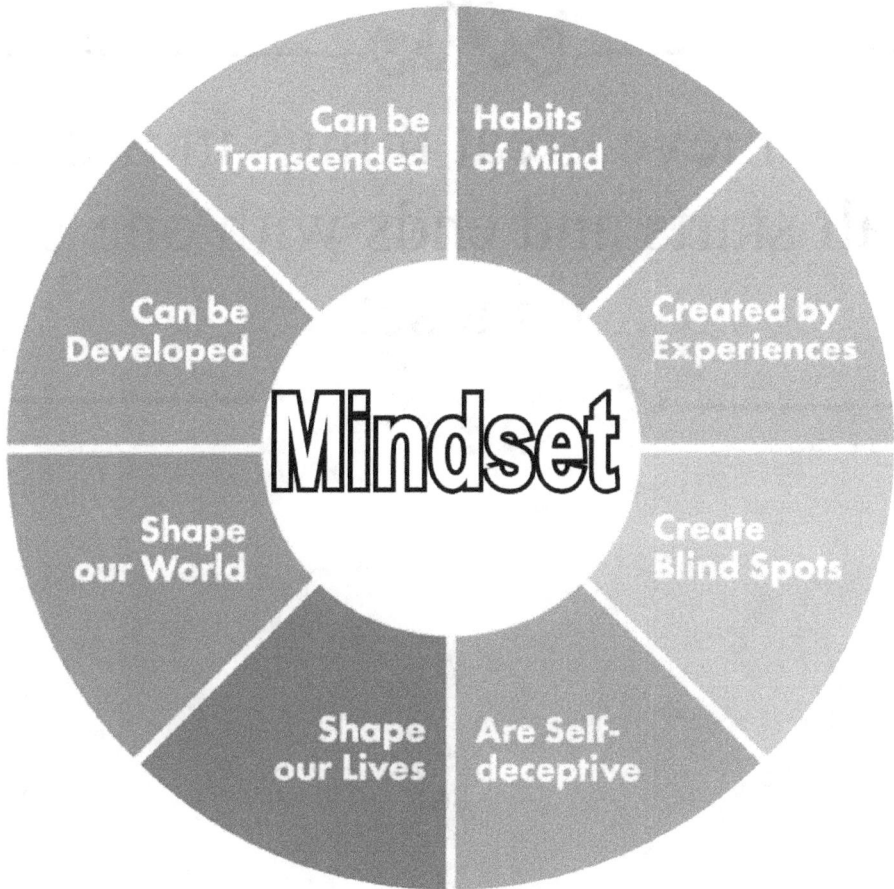

To achieve great things in life, it all starts and ends with one's mindset.

MINDSET

"That man is successful who has lived well, laughed often, and loved much – who has gained the respect of the intelligent men and the love of children – who has filled his niche and accomplished his task – who leaves the world better than he found it, whether by an improved poppy, a perfect poem or a rescued soul – who never lacked appreciation of earth's beauty nor failed to express it – who looked for the best in others and gave the best he had." Robert Louis Stevenson.

To achieve great things in life, it all starts and ends in one's mindset. If you have the right mindset towards things in life, it allows you to drive and focus on your dreams and actualize a lot of things. In my lifetime, I have experienced and passed through challenges that are strong enough to discourage me from moving on or chasing my dreams. But thank God for some beautiful books I read along the way, such as Rich Dad Poor Dad by Robert Kiyosaki and Success Through a Positive Mental Attitude by Napoleon Hill, to mention a few.

These fantastic books helped my thinking and reformed my way of seeing and doing things. These, in turn, helped me generate multiple income streams over the years. For one to gather knowledge that would transform your mindset, one needs to be very well informed by reading beautiful and educational books that enlighten and help your thinking. If your mindset is not channeled towards positivity and goalsetting, actualizing your dreams might be very hard to achieve.

All people in life have gone, are still going, and will still go through demanding challenges, and only the right mindset can help one come out valiant, be it emotional or financial. The mindset pushes you to keep going and never stop and helps you to move ahead in life after you have experienced heartbreak or economic relapse! This is simply because failing does not make you weak; falling and remaining down makes you vulnerable and seemingly defeated.

For everyone who has gone through different hard times, you owe yourself not to remain there but to pick yourself up and move on. So, you will have a good story to share when you become successful later in life. Some people might learn from it, become stronger and move on to be victorious.

Thomas Jefferson said, *"**Nothing** can stop **the** man with the right mental attitude from achieving his goal, and nothing on earth can help the man with **the** wrong **mental attitude to** move **ahead.**"*

I believe in myself; that is why I am strong enough to get to where I am today. I'm still on a journey of self-discovery, and many more potentials inside me need to be shared with the world. I know I am going to get there with time.

I also want to encourage you that you can do it, going through one challenge or the other. You can overcome it; you can achieve it. Get up and move, do not let that situation weigh you down. I am sure your story will be an inspiration to a lot of people out there tomorrow.

*Remember, a broken crayon can **still** give color.*

REFERENCES

Tireless mentors are a tangible
asset to humanity
while proudest and boasting
leaders are stigma in our society.

**Quotes and references and my gratitude for the following books
I read that made an impact on my life:**

******** *********

- Robert Kiyosaki   (*Rich Dad Poor Dad*)

- Napoleon Hill & W. Clement S. (*Success Through A Positive Mental Attitude*)

- Keith Harrell   (*Attitude is Everything*)

- Dale Carnagie   (*How To Win Friends And Influence People*)

- Robert Louis Stevenson   (Treasure Island)

- Lorrin L. Lee   (Make your life inspiring)

- Umberto Eco   (Author of the name of the rose)

ABOUT THE BOOK

"Learning thus not only consists of knowing what we must or can do but also knowing what we should do and perhaps shouldn't do." Umberto Eco said.

The Strength in me is a powerful motivational book engrossingly filled with educative guides to help you through some phases in life. It will give you a hunger and drive to go for your dreams alongside directing you on how to achieve them. It will enable you to look within to discover your inner potential and how to make use of it. If you are a dreamer and a believer, this book will enable you to build your confidence toward chasing those dreams, looking beyond all odds and challenges that may have hindered you from achieving your goals.

This is a book written from my personal experience and the experiences of friends and family. It is a book, friendly for all ages and races and gender. It's a book you will want to keep with you yet recommend to others to be a blessing to them.
In life, it's good to inspire others with your life's journey and how you conquered victoriously, so it can motivate others to win too.

ABOUT THE AUTHOR

Ozioma Juliet Anajekwu (nee Ekeocha) hails from Umu-Okpaa Egbelu Obube in Imo State, married to her heart-throb Mr. Ifeanyi George Anajekwu from Obiofia Umuenem in Nnewi North Anambra State, Nigeria. They are blessed with four wonderful children.
She attended Local Government Primary School, Shogunle, and Ikeja Grammar School, Bolade Oshodi, in Lagos, Nigeria. She went to ESUT (Enugu State University of Science and Technology) in Enugu, where she studied MME (Metallurgical and Materials Engineering) before moving to the U.S.A, New York City, where she finished as a Nurse Technician in 2001. She later returned to LASU (Lagos State University), finished with a B.A.Ed. in English Education, and graduated in 2016. She is a public speaker and a character-building coach for children. She owns a series of businesses and enjoys teaching.

www.ingramcontent.com/pod-product-compliance
Lightning Source LLC
Chambersburg PA
CBHW060515280326
41933CB00014B/2969